The Great Outdoor Camping Trip

Written by June Loves

Illustrated by Deborah Baldassi

ETA Cuisenaire

The Great Outdoor Camping Trip
ISBN 0-7406-1009-0
ETA 351041

Revised American edition published in 2004 by ETA/Cuisenaire®
under license from Era Publications. All rights reserved.

Text © June Loves
Illustrations © Deborah Baldassi

ETA/Cuisenaire Product Development Manager: Mary Watanabe
Lead Editor: Betty Hey
Editorial Team: Kevin Anderson, Kim O'Brien, Nancy Sheldon,
    Elizabeth Sycamore
Educational Consultant: Geraldine Haggard, Ed.D.

ETA/Cuisenaire • Vernon Hills, IL 60061-1862
800-445-5985 • www.etacuisenaire.com

Printed in China.

04 05 06 07 08 09 10 11 12 13   10 9 8 7 6 5 4 3 2 1

THE GREAT OUTDOOR CAMPING TRIP

Going camping with your family can be quite
an adventure. But camping outdoors in the
backyard was filled with more adventure than
this family had bargained for.

Once again, June Loves gets her readers
laughing — and the humor is in tents!

It was time for our vacation!
My little sister wanted to
go to the North Pole to find
a polar bear. Dad wanted to
go somewhere quiet to relax. I
wanted to go adventuring, and
Mom wanted to go camping.
Mom wanted to go on a Great
Outdoor Camping Trip.

Mom used to go camping in the great outdoors before she was a mother. Dad did not want to go camping. He has only been camping once in his whole life. That was when he met Mom. Dad said he was glad he met Mom, but he did not need to go camping again. In fact, he did not need to go on a Great Outdoor Camping Trip ever!

After a few days, we decided a Great Outdoor Camping Trip would be fun. Dad could find somewhere quiet to relax. I could find an adventure, and Lola might find a polar bear.

"You have to be organized to go camping," Dad said.

So, we made some lists.

Lola had our pets — Rufus, Fluffy, Tweetie, Flipper, and Squeaky — on her list. Dad made Lola take Rufus, Fluffy, Tweetie, Flipper, and Squeaky off her list.

"Pets can be a bit of a problem on a Great Outdoor Camping Trip," Dad said.

Tony-next-door said he would look after them for us. Tony is our very friendly neighbor.

Dad had on his list:
   golf gear
   fishing gear
   tennis gear
   books

I wanted to put on my list:
    deep-sea diving gear
    rock climbing gear
    helmet and parachute
But, I haven't got this stuff.
So, I just put:
    indoor games
    bat and baseball

Mom had important stuff on
her list:
   four sleeping bags
   mats and pillows
   a grill
   a table and four chairs
   a pan for washing
   a water container
   a cooler
   a lantern
   cups, plates, knives, and forks
   food and drinks
   four flashlights
   clothes and raincoats

Next, we needed a tent.

Dad wanted a big tent with three bedrooms, a kitchen, a dining room, a study, and a sunroom.

"Little tents are better. They are easy to put up and easy to take down," Mom said.

We found Mom's old tent in the shed.

We decided to go on our Great Outdoor Camping Trip on Friday, right after Dad came home from work.

19

On Friday, after school, we packed everything. Everything was all ready to be put into the car — just as soon as Dad arrived home from work.

Lola and I took our pets — Rufus, Fluffy, Tweetie, Flipper, and Squeaky — to Tony-next-door.

We were ready to go. We waited, and we waited, and we waited.

So, we took our camping gear into the backyard. It took a long time to unpack and set up our gear. Mom and Dad had forgotten how to put up a tent.

Mom made us promise — cross our hearts and hope to die — that we would not go inside the house for anything, except to go to the bathroom.

Lola and I went into Tony-next-door's house and brought

Rufus, Fluffy, Tweetie, Flipper, and Squeaky back home again. They were pleased to see us.

Mom and Dad said, "Fluffy and Rufus can come on our Great Outdoor Camping Trip, but it will be safer for Tweetie, Flipper, and Squeaky if they stay home."

We took Tweetie, Flipper, and Squeaky inside our house.

Then, Lola was hungry. Lola is always hungry. We unpacked the grill, but we couldn't light it. We'd forgotten the matches.

"I'm starving!" Lola cried.

Tony-next-door heard Lola. He popped up over the fence and gave us some matches.

Mom said this was OK because there are always friendly people who help each other when you are on a Great Outdoor Camping Trip.

29

We had baked beans, hot dogs, and chocolate milk for supper. Dad told us spooky stories until it got dark. It was a lot of fun!

Then, we went to bed — but didn't fall asleep.

In the dark, our backyard smelled different. And it sounded different. There were a lot of scary noises in our backyard. Rustling! Whistling! Crunching! Munching! And howling! Rufus was howling.

31

"Rufus is lonely," we said.

"OK," Dad said, "Rufus can come inside the tent with us."

We squeezed Rufus into the tent. We all agreed that Rufus could not help taking up so much room. It is not his fault that he is a very big, furry dog.

In the middle of the night, there was a big thud on the roof of our tent.

"It's a polar bear!" Lola said.

It wasn't. It was Fluffy, our cat.

"Fluffy is lonely. She wants to come in the tent with us," cried Lola.

"OK!" said Dad. "Fluffy can come inside the tent with us."

Then, Lola wanted to go to the bathroom. When Lola and Mom came back to the tent, they brought Flipper, Tweetie, and Squeaky with them.

"They were scared all by themselves in the house," Mom and Lola said.

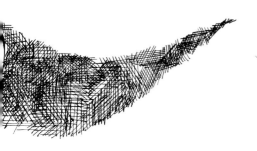

"OK!" said Dad. "They can come in the tent with us."

We found places in the tent to put Flipper's bowl, Tweetie's cage, and Squeaky's mouse house.

"Turn your flashlights off. Go to sleep!" said Mom and Dad.

Then, the wind began to blow. We heard thunder.

"Don't worry," said Mom. "It's only a summer storm. It will pass over quickly."

But, it didn't. It began to rain. The tent started to leak. It rained and it rained. Little streams of rain ran down from our saggy roof where Fluffy had jumped on it. The little streams of rain fell onto Dad's bed. They made little lakes on his sleeping bag.

We used our flashlights to find the little streams of rain. Our tent was leaking everywhere. Mom found our raincoats. We put cups and saucepans under the leaks and gave Dad an umbrella.

The wind blew and the rain pelted down.

"Rufus is scared! And Fluffy! And Flipper! And Tweetie! And Squeaky!" cried Lola. "They want to go home."

Our tent started to fill up with water.

"Let's go inside!" said Dad.

"What a good idea!" said our mother.

We carried Rufus, Fluffy, Tweetie, Flipper, and Squeaky inside.

We changed into dry clothes and Dad made hot chocolate.

"What an exciting camping trip!" Mom said. "Hasn't it been fun? Tomorrow when the tent is dry, we can find the holes and patch them! Then, the tent will be ready for our next Great Outdoor Camping Trip!"

"I want to go to Africa to find a lion," said Lola.

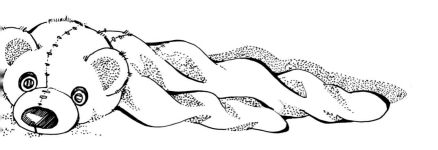

Dad and I looked at each other.

Dad and I think that if you don't have to go to school or work, staying at home is a fine vacation — especially if you don't camp in your own backyard!